More praise for
RISING VOICES

"The poems, brief essays, and testimonies convey a range of feelings, from pride in the old ways to conflict about the now. A few pieces flash with bitterness and attack white misconceptions. There's a heartbreaking early account by a Chippewa sent away to school for seven years, who came home a stranger. . . . It's the young people's words that will speak to readers about how it feels to be Indian trying to be in harmony with both ways."
—*Booklist*

"Always honest and heartfelt; expressing a variety of strong emotions with subtlety, simplicity, or irony but always with intelligence and conviction."
—*Kirkus Reviews* (starred review)

RISING VOICES

Writings of Young Native Americans

Selected by
Arlene B. Hirschfelder
and Beverly R. Singer

BALLANTINE BOOKS • NEW YORK

An Ivy Book
Published by The Random House Publishing Group

Copyright © 1992 by Arlene B. Hirschfelder and Beverly R. Singer

Published in the United States by Ivy Books, an imprint of The Random House Publishing Group, a division of Random House, Inc., New York, and simultaneously in Canada by Random House of Canada Limited, Toronto.

Ivy Books and colophon are trademarks of Random House, Inc.

www.ballantinebooks.com

Library of Congress Catalog Card Number: 91-32083

ISBN 0-8041-1167-7

This edition published by arrangement with Charles Scribner's Sons, an Imprint of Macmillan Publishing Company.

Manufactured in the United States of America

First Ballantine Books Edition: August 1993

OPM 29 28 27 26 25 24 23 22

To Mick Fedullo, who has encouraged Native American children to write.

—A.B.H.

To my parents, Jim and Bert Singer, and to other parents and teachers who have encouraged Native American children to write.

—B.R.S.

A portion of the authors' royalties will be donated to American Indian Science and Engineering Society (AISES) of Boulder, Colorado.

Contents

Foreword

"Get your facts straight," advises Katie Mobeck in her essay "Misconceptions about the Aleutians."

Indeed, Beverly R. Singer and I had this thought in mind when we selected pieces for this collection. Young Native Americans write volumes about everything, but we deliberately narrowed our selection to those poems and essays that set the record straight about their identity, their families, communities, rituals, histories, education, and harsh realities. Young people speak to these issues with intelligence, dignity, wit, and remarkable insight. Their words bear vivid, often eloquent witness to the realities of their lives over the past hundred years. They have much to tell us.

Arlene B. Hirschfelder

I was introduced to writing in my kindergarten classroom at the Bureau of Indian Affairs Day School in Santa Clara Pueblo, New Mexico, where the alphabet letters were purposely placed above the chalkboard. Penmanship, it seemed, was the final determinant of a student's overall ability to do well in school. Later came a host of individuals who inspired me to write because they wanted to share their knowledge and skills.

This opportunity to work with Arlene Hirschfelder was meant to happen so that readers might recognize, learn, and remember something of how American Indians experience life. These young writers and poets continue the Native life cycle: Like the rock inscriptions left by our earliest ancestors from the east to west coasts, they leave messages for the next generations. What is writing, after all? Indians write in much the same way and for similar reasons as anyone, but the content of our writing springs from memory, designs, songs, dances, dreams, and life evolving from a Native American past, present, and future.

Beverly R. Singer
(Santa Clara Pueblo)

Identity

Young people struggle with questions concerning their personal identity. They often ask themselves, "Who am I?" During this search, they doubt themselves; feel defective; challenge family and friends; suffer through moods, conflicting emotions, private yearnings, cosmic discontents; and agonize over the "who" they most want to be.

Indian teenagers struggle with the same who-am-I questions and suffer the same turmoil as all young people. They, too, must find their personal identity, but their search is more complicated than that of their non-Indian peers. Indians must learn to operate in a world that constantly rejects and attacks their Native cultures.

The writings that follow reveal young Indians intent on figuring out what it means to be Indian today, intent on confronting the ignorance, racist beliefs, and hatred that some other Americans heap on them—simply because they are identified as "Indian."

Uncertain Admission

The sky looks down on me in aimless blues
The sun glares at me with a questioning light
The mountains tower over me with uncertain shadows
The trees sway in the bewildered breeze
The deer dance in perplexed rhythms
The ants crawl around me in untrusting circles
The birds soar above me with doubtful dips and dives.
They all, in their own way, ask the question,
Who are you, who are you?
I have to admit to them, to myself,
I am an Indian.

Frances Bazil, a Coeur d'Alene, was a student in creative writing classes at the Institute of American Indian Arts in Santa Fe, New Mexico, when her poem won first prize in poetry in the under-sixteen category at the 1965 Scottsdale (Arizona) National Indian Arts Exhibition.

The Help Rain Gives Me

Rain falls down   ever gently
In the spring   sometimes.
And when it does
That's when I cry   for myself
Because I can't cry   before.
With the help of the rain falling   softly
Gentle crying relieves me.
It lessens the pain   the rush of
Harsh, everyday living   worrying.
People think me strange   weird
When they see me walking
No cover   bare arms   bare head.
To soft, gentle spring's teardrops
I add my own   But
People don't know why I do that
And I never tell them
They wouldn't understand,   nor try to,
Just put me in a little cubbyhole
In their minds   label me
"Strange   weird   cries in the rain."
They can't understand   for
They're not capable of that
Always too worried   too hurried
Can't ever know   how clean I feel

Cry
Crying in the rain.

In 1970, Ethel Patkotak, an Inuit, was in a tenth-grade creative writing class at Mount Edgecumbe High School in Alaska, a school run by the Bureau of Indian Affairs (BIA). Her contest-winning poem was screened first at her school before being submitted to judges of the Creative Writing Project, established to provide American Indian students with opportunities to express themselves in writing. Her poem was published in 1970 in Arrow II.

I'm a Navajo

I'm a Navajo, and I don't act like a Navajo. . . . A Navajo is a person who wears lots of necklaces and belts and pins made by Navajo silversmiths. And I don't even have a pin to put on my dress or a necklace to show my people that I am a Navajo on Indian day.

Navajo ladies wear their necklaces to show that they are Navajos. And they wear their knots or buns on their head. But my hair is long and I don't wear knots.

Navajos live in hogans. But I don't live in a hogan like my grandmom did. My mom never did have a hogan of her own. I wish she did, for I like the Navajo traditional ways, but I'm not fit for them now.

My grandmom was taught how to pray in Navajo ways when she was just a little girl. But I was taught how to pray in white ways. Now I have to take Navajo history in class, to learn all my old people's ways, the traditional ways, the Navajo ways. My grandfather once knew all about the sacred mountains. But now he is gone.

I don't even know a thing about the sacred mountains. All I know is that once they were very holy to my people and meant a lot to them in prayers. I have respect for my people and the traditional ways. I am a Navajo.

6

These excerpts are from an essay written by Maggie Bahe, a Navajo student at Wingate High School in Fort Wingate, New Mexico, in 1971. The essay appeared in the school's monthly publication, Shush Da Bizaad.

Indian

Being Indian is . . .
eating wild rice and seeds.

Being Indian is . . .
having Indian and white friends,
but still being called apple.

Being Indian is . . .
having prejudiced teachers,
but them not admitting it.

Being Indian is . . .
being sensitive about all the broken
            treaties and massacres.

Being Indian is . . .
admiring some of your white friends' clothes.

Being Indian is . . .
going without new shoes or a good coat
that school year
'cause your mom and dad didn't get in
            enough ricing.

Being Indian is . . .
knowing how to talk
  Indian until you start school.

Being Indian is . . .
watching TV and crying along with an
                Indian
after a man just drove by and threw a
bag of garbage at his feet.

Being Indian is . . .
having dolls like Buffy St. Marie and Dennis Banks.

[Buffy St. Marie is a Cree songwriter, singer, and actor.
Dennis Banks is a Chippewa political activist.]

*Glory Thompson, an Ojibway (or Chippewa) from the
Fond du Lac Reservation, wrote this poem when she
attended the Cloquet Junior High School in Minnesota.
It was published in the* Native American Class Newspaper *in December of 1971.*

Longing

My soul longs for freedom,
To be free as an eagle
That soars the sky.
My soul thirsts for my tribal ways,
It longs for the tribal beliefs,
Which are so dear to my heart.
If I can only be free,
Be free to exist,
To be me.
I am Indian in a confusing world,
In a world that won't let me be free.
Oh, how I long for my freedom.

This poem was written by Renae Kemp, a Choctaw-Chickasaw student in the twelfth grade in Classen High School in Oklahoma City, Oklahoma, as part of a Language Arts unit developed by educators and students from the Oklahoma City and Tulsa schools. It was published in The Oklahoma Indian American School Guide, *1979.*

A Trail Not Yet Finished

Standing here in my red-dyed
moccasin
my sole is worn to dark gray
showing that I have walked about
the earth for some time
my trail is set for you
walk in my trails my son
there are curves in it but
please walk it straight with pride
proudness of mine and yours
dignity will pave the way of
your trail
a trail of nature
   a trail of grandma
      a trail of mine
         a trail for my children
            a trail for generations
               to come
Be proud and respected as a
person, be proud in what you
are and what you may
become in the future.

Priscilla Badonie, a Navajo student at Rough Rock
Community High School in Arizona, wrote "A Trail Not

Yet Finished" for an English assignment. It was published in 1983 in Rough Stones Are Precious Too, Vol. 3, *a publication of the Navajo Curriculum Center at the school.*

To Be an Indian

Being Indian today is what you as an Indian make of it. You can live the traditional ways of yesterday or you can blend in with today's white society. But remember, you cannot wash the color of your skin away. But you can wash the pride of being Indian away, only if you as an Indian want to.

To me, being Indian is the same, but being in a different environment. You "have to" get an education today. Yesterday, you "had to" fill your quiver with arrows. Today, you "have to" fill your head with knowledge. Yesterday, you "had to" hunt and gather food. You "had to" set up camp and have strong, steady poles. Today, you "have to" get a job, pay bills, buy food, rent or buy a home.

But today it's much easier. You have welfare, food stamps, handouts. And you have alcohol. Yet, it's much harder.

If you can survive in today's society and maintain your *soul* self, and if you can do these things and know who you are as a person, you are a true warrior.

In 1984, the Red School House in St. Paul, Minnesota, sponsored a poetry and essay contest. Murray

Stonechild, Cree, a graduate of the Red School House, won second place for his essay. The winning entries were published in Ikway, *a magazine about Indian women.*

My Poems

I am a sun poet
sitting on a ray
of streaming light
writing
gold poems.
Quickly, my poems
shine down on
the earth
and hide
in grains of
burning sand.

I am a rain poet
under an old
gray umbrella
finishing wet, soggy
poems. As I finish,
my poems slowly
run away
and slide in
alleys and streets
of huge cities.

I am a sea poet
riding a sea

turtle while
writing poems.
My poems slither away
and have fun
swimming with fish
in the green, dark
waters.

I am a building poet
on the roof
writing poems.
My poems run into cracks
in walls
and cry out
to me.

I am a space poet
riding on a
falling star.
My poems fly
off
in the cold darkness
and are lost
forever in
twisting mysterious galaxies.

Alan Barlow, a Navajo from the Utah Navajo Reserva-tion, wrote "My Poems" during sixth grade. They were published in 1986 in A House of Clouds, *an anthology of poetry by students of the Montezuma Creek and Mex-ican Hat elementary schools in Utah. It was edited by Lorraine Ferra, a poet with the Utah Arts Council.*

As I Walk along the Hillside

As I walk along the hillside,
I think about who my ancestors were
and how they lived.

I see tepees, and smoke
rising from them; the dry-meat poles
are filled,

buffalo hides being tanned,
children laughing, playing,
old men telling stories,
and young men become
warriors.
I hear the sound of drums beating

and people singing, dancing, eating.
I see horses grazing
on green grass in the meadow,
and as I walk along the hillside
I feel all these things inside me,
helping me to be who I am.

*Misty Stands in Timber, a Northern Cheyenne student
in sixth grade in Lame Deer, Montana, wrote "As I
Walk along the Hillside" while she was in a creative*

writing class taught by Mick Fedullo, a poet who has developed lessons in poetry writing for students in grades five through nine. Misty's poem was published in the 1987–1988 Lame Deer School Poetry Calendar.

Under One Sun

The early morning, overcast and quiet,
found me walking alone on a side of a ridge.
I stopped to gaze
over the valleys and canyons.
As I looked, I wondered how my ancestors lived.
The wind that blew around me sounded like drums
beating at a powwow.
I started to realize the meaning of this series of beats.
After a while, I started to hum
to the beats. Then all of a sudden
it went away.
While walking home, I realized
how much I needed to hold on to
my culture.

[Powwows are social events at which there is dancing, singing, drumming, and feasting.]

Neal Beaumont, a Crow student from Montana, wrote "Under One Sun" when he was in the tenth grade. It was published in 1990 in an anthology called A Tree Full of Leaves Which Are Stars, *edited by Mick Fedullo. The anthology brings together Native American student poetry written on many reservations throughout the West.*

My Role as a Native American

I was fifteen years old when I auditioned for the school play *The Wizard of Oz*. I wasn't counting on a main role, maybe a munchkin because of my height. I am four feet nine inches, have dark skin, and black hair. If there was any role in this play that I would not fit, it was the tall, white, blond, beautiful Glinda the Good Witch. But that was the role I received. I was so humiliated. I thought it was a joke, and there was no way that I was going to play Glinda and be the joke of the school. But a very good friend of mine changed my mind. It was in this artificial role that I realized that this society needed a change. Although Glinda was the stereotypical beautiful white goddess, I was given the opportunity to reverse this role. I didn't need the looks on the outside; it didn't matter. I had what counted, what was inside. I made this play a part of my real life.

Now, if there is a hurdle of any sort, if I don't necessarily fit the society's role, I fight for what I believe to be equal. Like Billy Mills and Chief Joseph, I want the Native American people, including my family, to be proud of me; but more importantly, I would like to be proud of myself. . . .

I believe my role as a Native American is to fight our stereotype and show others that all people are truly equal.

[Billy Mills, an Oglala Lakota (Sioux), is the renowned athlete who, during the Tokyo games in 1964, became the first and only American to win an Olympic gold medal in the 10,000-meter run. Chief Joseph, born in 1840, led his people, the Nez Percés, over sixteen hundred miles in their attempt to escape from the United States military in 1877. For almost three months, Chief Joseph and his group, in some of the finest battle strategy ever witnessed, fought off United States military commands over a dozen times. They were about thirty miles from the Canadian border when winter conditions became so severe that Chief Joseph, not wanting the remaining Nez Percés to freeze or starve to death, surrendered to General Nelson A. Miles on October 5, 1877.]

In 1987, Kimberly Kai Rapada, a Nooksack senior at Bainbridge High School on Bainbridge Island, Washington, wrote the preceding essay about herself when she applied for a scholarship from the Adolph Van Pelt Foundation.

I Have a Dream

I Have a Dream
That the world is peaceful,
That people stopped fighting in the night.
I wish that war was not invented.

I Have a Dream
That my family is together
Forever, until we grow up
And can take care of our own selves.

I Have a Dream
That I am the best reader in my class,
And the fastest runner.

Craig Magpie, from Santa Clara Pueblo in New Mexico, wrote his poem during third grade at Santa Clara Day School. The students chose selections from the year's work, typed them on a classroom computer with the help of teacher Robin Rodar, and produced a 1990 calendar.

Family

The most durable and resilient American Indian social unit is the family. The role of the Indian family, like that of any family, is to pass on the values, attitudes, and beliefs of the community at large. The family exposes children to life-cycle rituals and ceremonial events, and in doing so contributes to the knowledge and understanding of the next generation, which insures there will be another generation of Indians to pass this information on.

Native families today have to one degree or another moved away from the traditional practices of extended-family living arrangements. Single-family homes are available on reservations; moreover, many families now live in urban communities apart from their relatives on the reservation. As Native Americans deal with the demands of everyday living and self-sufficiency, family bonds have weakened, but the family still remains the core from which children learn about Indian lifeways. For many Indians, knowing who they are and where their families come from is extremely important. This knowledge is the basis for one's identity and helps one live with a purpose.

Often, the gentlest and kindest people in a Native family are held in high esteem, and they are usually one's grandparents. They are typically memorialized through songs and rituals.

Shi-ma-sani and Shi-cheeh

I was born in a hogan. Shi-ma-sani raised me. She let my hair grow long and made my Navajo bun.

She made me long silk skirts and velveteen blouses, decorated with buttons made by Shi-cheeh. She taught me how to make fry-bread, take care of sheep, and use mutton for food.

Shi-cheeh would sing over me when I was sick. Shi-cheeh made me nice jewels, which I wear to the ceremonies, and he made moccasins for me. Shi-cheeh told me lots of stories, taught me how to sing, pray, and hand-tremble.

I'm proud and happy that Shi-ma-sani and Shi-cheeh taught me a lot of things.

[*Shi-ma-sani* is the Navajo word for grandmother. *Shi-cheeh* is the Navajo word for grandfather.]

Peggy Yazzie, a Navajo student, wrote this essay about her grandmother and grandfather in 1971 for Shush Da Bizaad, *the monthly publication at Wingate High School in Fort Wingate, New Mexico.*

Gah-Chac-Ah

Grandmother, aged in beauty,
Hands wrinkled and soft.
I knew no other so kind.

Cecil Johnson, Jr., a Pima from Arizona who was a senior at Phoenix Indian High School, published this poem in 1971 in Arrow III. *His poem was screened at his school before being submitted to judges of the Creative Writing Project sponsored by the Bureau of Indian Affairs (BIA) and directed by T. D. Allen. The BIA-funded project provided American Indian students with opportunities to express themselves in writing.*

Grammas Are Good

Grammas are good
>they're soft
>they're clean and not clean
>they smell good and not good
>they tell stories
>they make quilts

*Virgil Yellow Cloud, an Oglala Lakota (Sioux), wrote
this poem when he was eleven years old and in the fourth
grade at the Porcupine Day School on the Pine Ridge
Indian Reservation in South Dakota. His poem was selected for inclusion in a 1971 exhibition organized by the
U.S. Department of the Interior Indian Arts and Crafts
Board. It was also included in* Photographs and Poems
by Sioux Children from the Porcupine Day School, *the
exhibition catalog.*

A Visit to Grandmother

One summer afternoon when I went to visit Grandmother, she was busy with her pottery. She was sitting
on the floor on her green shawl, with her pottery all
around her. In her hand was a small bowl, which she
was polishing.

I sat beside Grandmother to watch her smooth and
polish the pottery. To smooth out the rough edges, she
used a Choregirl. Then, dampening the pottery, she
rubbed it with a small, smooth stone until it shone.

Her hands at times would move swiftly and then slow
down. While working, she sometimes hummed a song
to herself. As I was sitting beside Grandmother, she
didn't even glance at me for a long time because she
was concentrating on her pottery.

After polishing the pottery, she then was ready to
paint her designs. The different kinds of designs mean
different things to the Tewa tribe. One of the many she
painted represented a bird flying in the rain. The light
and dark brown colors of the designs blended harmo-
niously with the tannish background.

While painting, she frequently dipped her small yucca
brush into the paint, which was inside a stone that was
broken in half. More concentration was needed in painting than in polishing. Her hands moved very slowly.

Grandmother was so quiet that one would not know that she was still working.

After completing the painting, she glanced up at me over her eyeglasses and asked, "When did you come?"

I said, "I came a long time ago."

Then we both laughed and sat there on the floor chatting for a few minutes. She then arose and put her pottery on a shelf in a safe spot where it would remain until she was ready to bake it.

Soon afterward I left for home. As I walked down the mesa, I was thinking of how great it is to have a grandmother like her. Being around her makes me proud to have such a wonderful person to be with and to talk to.

Vernida Polacca, a Hopi Tewa, wrote this essay during eleventh grade at the Phoenix Indian School in Arizona. The essay was originally published in 1972 in Arrow IV, *one of four collections of contest-winning prose and poetry edited by T. D. Allen, project director for a special writing program conducted in numerous schools operated by the Bureau of Indian Affairs.*

Susan

My grandma is old and gone.
I remember her a little.
She sat in her wheelchair
like a stone; she sat there
waving like a tree, but just a little.
She was 107 years old when she died.
She had a wrinkled face when she smiled.
She knew a lot but didn't talk.
I would try to think what she
was thinking about.
Her family had a powwow for her
right in the hospital living room.
She must have been happy that day.
She had gray hair and sad eyes.
I think her name was Susan.
But she is happy now,
where she is.

Thomas Headbird, a Chippewa from Cass Lake, Minnesota, wrote this poem while a student at Bug-O-Nay-Ge-Shig Day School. The poem was featured in the 1979 publication Angwamas Minosewag Anishinabeg: Time of the Indian, *a project sponsored by COMPAS (Community Programs in the Arts and Sciences) and the Minnesota Chippewa Tribe.*

Gifts

My grandma gave
me her little
dress that she used

to wear when she was
little. My grandpa
gave me the part

of land that he
owned. My father
gave me his best horse

before he passed away.
Now I still have the
horse. Whenever I feed

or ride the horse, I think
of my father. When I
wear the dress my grandma

gave to me I think of
her. My grandpa gave me
part of his land. I always

clean and plant on it.
These things were blessed first.

*This poem by Michelle Whatoname, a Havasupai, was
included in* The Eye of a White Dove, *a collection of
student poems from the Havasupai Elementary School
in Arizona, edited by Mick Fedullo and published in
1985. The "Supai" students live at the bottom of the
Grand Canyon along the Colorado River.*

As I Dance

As I dance with the drum
I see my feathers and the elk teeth
on my dress. They look
like bells ringing. My grandmother
sees me dancing with
the beat of the drum. She remembers
when she was little, used to dance.
She feels good about me,
and I am glad I am Indian and
taking on the heritage of the Crow people.

*Autumn White Clay, a fifth-grade Crow student from
Montana, wrote "As I Dance" after working with Mick
Fedullo, poet-in-residence at her school. The poem appears in* Where Does the Moon Go?, *an anthology published in 1986.*

About Grandma

The old lady is sitting
outside the hogan
weaving a rug,
with her white hair
going back and forth
in the air as the wind
goes by very slow,
her fingers moving like
the legs of a spider,
with her mind full
of the things that she
did before she got old,
and her mind on the rug,
forgetting all about
the things she planned
to do for the day, and her
eyes just moving upon the wind.

Benjamin Hunch, a Navajo, wrote about his grand-mother while he was at Wingate Elementary School in New Mexico. His poem was published in the 1987–1988 Wingate Elementary School Poetry Calendar, *edited by Mick Fedullo.*

Grandpa

His eyes glow like pearls in the water
sitting like a majestic eagle
staring into nothing—
dusty old hat
that's seen many years.

Knobby old cane shines in the sun;
he walks through the small
sand canyon which once was flat.
The lizard bows to the aging man
for soon he will be gone
like the lady he loves.

Cars zooming by like a trail of ants—
the sound of kids playing
like the sound of a storm
he only can hear—
the thought of the years.

Shandin Pete, a Salish-Kootenai, wrote this poem as an eighth-grade student, while he participated in a creative writing project at Arlee Junior High School in Arlee, Montana, conducted by Mick Fedullo, a poet-in-residence. The poem was published in 1988 in Behind a Blue Cotton Mountain.

My Late Grandfather

Once my grandfather
herded sheep back to
the corral. He could see
the sun throwing its
sunbeams into the blue sky.

He chopped wood and
brought it home on the back
of an old pickup truck.

As he drove home he thought
about how hard the work was.
He remembered his father telling him about
the long-past wars. Enemy tribes
would make war on the Navajos.

Even though he thought
he should run
early in the morning.

It was no use,
he was too old. Finally home
and opening the door,
he could see his wrinkles
in a mirror from a distance.

Wearing his old clothes, he
walked into the hogan.

Now, he is buried
in the Mother Earth, with his
turquoise bracelet and his rings.

Elliot Bryant, a Navajo, wrote "My Late Grandfather"
during fifth grade. It was published in 1990 in A Tree
Full of Leaves Which Are Stars, *a collection of Native*
American student poems collected and edited by Mick
Fedullo. The anthology is a compilation of writings re-
sulting from Mr. Fedullo's poetry workshops with Native
students throughout the West over the past several years.

My Family

My mom is by the table, beading a belt.
My dad is sitting, watching the television.
My two brothers are playing basketball outside.
My oldest sister is out on a date.
My second-oldest sister is reading a book.
My little sister is out visiting our cousins.
I'm asleep on the couch!
I'm able to sleep
because I know my family is all around me.

Delia Spotted Bear, an eighteen-year-old student from the Crow Tribe in Montana, wrote this poem in 1990 while at Haskell Indian Junior College in Lawrence, Kansas. She took creative writing classes with Denise Low.

My Grandfather

My grandfather's name was Bob Henry. I never knew him, but in our home he will live forever because of the memories my dad and mom have. Some things are much better than television, and stories of my grandfather are great. You see, he was a medicine man. He used herbs, roots, and magic. People still talk about his medicine even though he has been dead for years. He passed on many tales and legends to us, one of which I will share with you.

This legend begins with a young Choctaw boy who hated cruelty to animals, especially the deer. This boy felt very close to the deer and he felt the pain of their loved ones being killed. He prayed to the Great Spirit, asking for help to save the deer. He told the Great Spirit he was willing to dedicate his life to this cause.

This boy went to sleep. When he awoke, he was half deer, half boy with the screech of an old woman. When the hunters came, he would run through the woods and screech, scaring them away. It has been said that even to this day, if a person is hunting deer on Choctaw land, he may encounter the half deer, half boy with an old woman's screech.

James Henry, a sixteen-year-old Mississippi Choctaw student, wrote this essay about his grandfather in 1991 for an English assignment. The Mississippi Choctaws are located in east-central Mississippi.

Homelands

The beauty of being an American Indian is realized through an affinity and love for the land from which one comes. It is this simple, yet complex, idea that makes it difficult for some to understand why Indians continue to hold steadfastly to their reservation lands and do battle with non-Indians, the federal government, and sometimes with each other over land ownership.

The writings in this section are an affirmation of identity that Native Americans develop about their homelands from birth. Even if they have never seen their reservations because circumstances prevent them from living there, or they no longer have a reservation, as many Indians lost their land centuries earlier, they recognize their ancestors' place of birth as their own.

Native people experience a feeling of belonging to their land. It's the place where they feel completely free to experience all the senses at once. It is the place many will return to at the end of life if they have been away from home most of their lives.

For centuries, American Indian people have lived competently and completely from what the earth provided for them. The knowledge and skills acquired for living this way still exist in pockets on many reservations. Reliance on this older knowledge is important for survival.

My Tribe

I am a Zuni Indian boy. I live in a Zuni village. The Zuni village is south of Gallup, New Mexico. It is forty-four miles from Gallup.

The Zuni houses are made of adobe bricks and some are made of stones. They build square houses. They usually have four or five rooms.

There is a mountain on the east side of the village. It is called Thunder Mountain. Once when there was a big flood, all the Zunis went to Thunder Mountain to save themselves from the big flood. The water almost reached the top of the mountain. The priest's daughter and his son were thrown into the water; that is why the water stopped instead of just keeping on going up. The water went down slowly and there are mountains with white marks around them where the water stopped for a while. We can still see the marks around the mountains. A girl and a boy had changed into two rocks. We can still see these two rocks on Thunder Mountain. They are on the west side of the mountain.

The climate is pleasant. It is not so hot in summer as it is here in Phoenix, Arizona. It is cold in wintertime. The temperature is often ten degrees below zero.

James Latone, a Zuni from New Mexico, wrote about his tribe while he was a student at the Phoenix Indian

School in Arizona, a boarding school operated by the Bureau of Indian Affairs until its closing in 1989. His article appeared in The Phoenix Redskin, *the school newspaper, on December 3, 1932.*

It Is Not!

The Navajo Reservation a lonesome place?
It is Not!
The skies are sunny,
Clear blue,
Or gray with rain.
Each day is gay—
In Nature's way.
It is not a lonesome place at all.
A Navajo house shabby and small?
It is Not!
Inside there's love,
Good laughter,
And *Big Talk*.
But best—
It's home
With an open door
And room for all.
A Castle could have no more.

*"It Is Not!" was composed by a fifth-year group in the
Special Navajo Program in 1940. It appeared in* The
New Trail, *the Phoenix Indian School yearbook, in 1953.*

Bison

Where has he gone?
The great shaggy beast.
The wild one.
The provider,
The warmth from cold.
The food to drive away hunger.
The robe and moccasins for my feet.
The leather for my shirt.
The skin for my tent.
The bones for my tools.
The sinew for my bowstring.
The horn for my spoon and cups.
The stomach for a bag to carry my things in.
The rawhide.
I look for him on the plains and he is not there.
I look for him in the meadows and the valleys
        and at the water and
he is not there either.
I cannot live without him.

Tonye Garter, a Cheyenne River Sioux, wrote this poem while a senior at Cheyenne Eagle Butte High School in South Dakota. It was published in 1971 in Arrow III, *one of four volumes of contest-winning writings of Native American students from across the United States.*

The four volumes were edited by T. D. Allen, project director for a special writing program sponsored by the Bureau of Indian Affairs.

As I Walk This Road

As I walk this road I hear
the laughter of the new season
coming forth.

I see the green as it makes its way
through the white snowy blanket
as it greets the morning sun.

The sun is gone now
and soon will appear again
to see the new colors of a new season
when the sap will flow.

As the last of the rice is put away,
and as we give thanks for a good harvest
it is time to cover our mother
with a white blanket
so she may rest.

Ricardo Rojas, a Chippewa from the White Earth Reservation who grew up in the Minneapolis-St. Paul area of Minnesota, wrote this poem while enrolled at the Red School House. He participated in a special writing project designed to encourage creative writing by young Native Americans, sponsored by COMPAS (Community

Programs in the Arts and Sciences) and the Minnesota Chippewa Tribe. The poem was published in 1979 in Angwamas Minosewag Anishinabeg: Time of the Indian.

A Message

The wind had a message, the sun had a message, the sky had a message. All I had to do was listen. I'm at the top of a rocky hill listening to all sorts of sounds that surround me. As I listen to these sounds of the wind blowing, the hot sun is shining, the sky is all cool, blue colored like an ocean. The wind is blowing very slow, the sun ray is also sending messages to me. It seems like it is sending a kind of message only I shall know. A message that's good for me to know. It tells me of how things were in the past:

About when the Indians went to Fort Sumner. All the quietness and peacefulness explain the way the Indians finally settled down on the land, living and communicating with nature, as my grandmother did so long ago. She was little at that time, when she and the rest of our people were forced to go to Fort Sumner. Many had died along the way from sickness and hunger, after they had spent five years at the fort using and eating what was given to them. At last they were released, happy and longing to get back to their land.

As the treaties were signed, our people thought they had nothing to fear as long as they were on their own land. They believed the earth was their mother. It gave them all they needed, such as plants and trees to build homes; it protected them from danger. The plants were in different varieties which they ate. Water came from the earth so they wouldn't get thirsty. The warm sun gave them warmth. The land was their true home where they belonged. They felt close to the land, not only because the land gave them food and drink, but because it gave them strength. The fresh air and other natural elements gave them strength. It gave them a reason to go on and live.

They are very thankful for all these things and not once did it lie or make a fool out of them. It always gave them something to continue on. For all these things they thanked the earth in their own ceremonial prayers. To this day it still hasn't changed. Our people are thankful for what the earth gave us. And our love for the earth hasn't changed at all.

Jennifer Yazzie, a Navajo student at Rough Rock Community High School in Arizona, wrote this essay during the 1977–1978 school year. It appeared in 1982 in Rough Stones Are Precious Too, *Vol. 2, published by the Navajo Curriculum Center at the school.*

As I See

As I see an old Pima
woman walking across the
freshly watered land, I
think about how beautiful
the land is.

I think of how it once was
long ago. As I drift
into the multicolored past,
I am changing. I am changing
into a cactus.

As I stand so still in the
hot orange sun, I watch
as people build villages
around me. I watch in
joy as the children play.

As the dark clear night
falls, I drift to sleep and
back into the present time.
The old woman is gone,
and now I am alone.

Jessica Ahmsaty, a Pima, author of "As I See," partic-
ipated in a special writing program at the Sacaton School
on the Gila River Indian Reservation in Arizona. She
and her fellow students worked with Mick Fedullo, a
poet-in-residence, and published their poetry in 1983 in
Adobe Sings, *an anthology in which each poem is trans-*
lated into the Pima language.

We Are the Many

We are the people of long ago.
We are the blue-green water
       that runs swiftly in the creek.
We are the flowers which blossom
       in the spring.
We are the rain that comes pouring
       down in the canyon.
We are the lightning
       that streaks in the sky.
We are the cottonwood trees
       that loom high into the air.
We are the gentle breeze of the many winds.
We are the blood of the mighty warriors.
We are the ancestors of the Havasupai children.

Ingrid Putesoy, a Havasupai student at the Havasupai Elementary School, wrote this poem, published in 1985 in The Eye of a White Dove.

Canyons

        Canyons, Echoing
going away—coming back
        repeating my voice

Andrew Jones, a Navajo, was eleven years old when he composed his haiku. The poem was selected for a 1985 "contest issue" of Beads and Ribbons, *a publication of the Montezuma Creek Arts Council in cooperation with the Montezuma Creek Elementary School, which is on the Utah strip of the Navajo nation. Bruce Hucko served as the advisor for the publication.*

Misconceptions about the Aleutians

The public has many misconceptions about the Aleutian region's geography and culture. Most informed people could locate the Aleutian chain, but that's about it. Most Americans think that all Native Alaskans are Eskimos: That's wrong. Some think we live on an iceberg. Few know of the Aleuts. The Aleuts are one of the three major Alaska Native groups, but the one that is least known. The distinction between Eskimo, Indian, and Aleut can be described in terms of their arrival in Alaska. . . .

The influence of external events on the Aleuts has been great. Even the name of our people has a foreign source. The Aleutian Aleuts called themselves *Unangan*, meaning, "the people." At the time that the Russians arrived in 1741 there were about sixteen thousand Aleuts. The Russians killed and enslaved the Aleuts; within one hundred years there were only about two thousand.

Nevertheless, we're still here, and things have changed a lot since then, particularly since World War II. We live in standard, well-furnished homes, and we never lived in igloos. At the time of Russian contact, we did live in *barabaras*: partially underground, sod houses large enough for several families. Since the islands are treeless, driftwood was used for the frame and roof beams. Whale bones were also used to frame.

I am most familiar with the communities around the western tip of the Alaska peninsula. The economy of these communities depends primarily on commercial fishing. They are Sand Point, King Cove, and Nelson Lagoon. There is a substantial Aleut population in each of these three communities. Families in each community are related to families in the other two. Most people of Aleut descent in these communities have Scandinavian or Russian surnames. Scandinavians came to the Aleutians as crew members on fishing vessels, stayed, and later took Aleut wives.

Some small, less accessible Aleut villages without the advantages of a sustained cash economy have been abandoned. Over the years, the communities of Pavlof and Squaw Harbor on Sanak Island and Belkofski on the peninsula have been abandoned in favor of King Cove, Sand Point, and other communities.

Most think we are knee-deep in snow all year. Actually there is only two to six weeks of snow coverage per year. The Aleutians have a maritime climate characterized by mild winters and cool summers. The average daily temperatures in Adak range from twenty-nine to thirty-eight degrees in the winter and from forty-one to fifty-six degrees in the summer. These temperatures greatly contrast with mean temperatures of Alaska's interior. . . . The Aleutians lie between the fifty-first and fifty-fifth parallels, which is the same latitude as that of England and south of Norway and Denmark.

Food is another source of misunderstanding; some

people think the primary food of all Alaska Native people is whale, walrus, and seal. That's wrong, too. Once sea mammals were essential to the Aleut diet. When sea mammal is available, it is still prepared and eaten in a few communities, but not in those with which I am familiar. Around the tip of the peninsula, commercial fishing has converted us from a subsistence economy to a cash economy; nevertheless, fish and game are important to our diet. We eat a lot of caribou, duck, geese, and salmon. When they are available we have crab and shellfish. We buy pork, fowl, and lots of beef. Although the meat is often not that familiar to an outsider, the menu is usually very American. Today we routinely eat well-known American food such as hamburgers and fries and bacon and eggs, but the hamburger may be half caribou.

So, most Americans need to change their perceptions about the Aleutians and its people. Get your facts straight.

Katie Mobeck, an Aleut from Alaska, wrote this piece about her people when she was a twelfth-grade student in Nelson Lagoon. It was published in 1986 in the fifth volume of Taniisix, *a writing project begun in 1979 that involved students of the Aleutian Region School District in a cultural journalism program.*

The Navajo Land

The Navajo land is covered
with trees, weeds, and animals.
It has canyons and big mountains.
The Navajos fought, suffered, and died
on this land. The Navajos long ago
prayed to keep the land which
we have now.

The Navajos hunted across
this sacred land to keep in good health,
and they danced and sang on this land.
But most of all, we love
our Navajo land.

*Willis Belin, a Navajo student at Wingate Elementary
School in Fort Wingate, New Mexico, had his poem pub-
lished in the* 1987–1988 Wingate Elementary School
Poetry Calendar.

The Bighorn River

The Bighorn River flows
through the reservation.
As it goes, it meets the
Little Bighorn. They are like
a big brother and a little
brother together.

The sound of it makes
the reservation special.
It seems as if it protects
the reservation with happiness
and care. The reservation
knows it has a close friend
and that's the river.

The river wants to flow
to all the four winds but
knows it can just flow one way
with the same wind.

*Len Plenty, a member of the Crow Tribe in Montana,
wrote his poem during sixth grade. He worked with Mick
Fedullo, poet-in-residence at the Crow Agency and Fort*

Smith Elementary School. "The Bighorn River" was published in 1988 in Swinging in the Wind, *an anthology of student poetry.*

Yaqui Hopes

I look down from
a high cloud. I see
Yaqui women cooking
Yaqui food, and men
chopping wood for the
fire for the women
to cook, and the
kids running around
waiting for the
food, and
cool air blowing
the beautiful smell
to my face, and
the trees' leaves
falling down
one after another.
I hope that it
will be
like this forever.

Glafiro Perez, a Yaqui, was in the sixth grade at Richey Elementary School at Old Pascua Yaqui Village in Arizona when he wrote "Yaqui Hopes." He participated in a special writing program sponsored by ArtsReach, a Tucson-based organization that was founded to help build American Indian students' academic skills and confidence in imaginative writing. The poem was published in 1990 in Dancing with the Wind: The Arts-Reach Literary Magazine, *Vol. 2.*

Apache People and Their Heritage

Proud of their ways.

The Crown Dancers
Weaving a path
around the flickering
fire,

tossing their shadows
to the dancing
people.

song which
floats above the
sky

into the
heavens;

the swishing
sound of
leather,

and the silvery
sound of
tinsels,

feathers and
beads on
clothes,

made by the
proud Apache
people

trying to live
like they once
did

long ago.

Lillian Rainer, a San Carlos Apache/Taos Pueblo, wrote her poem during eighth grade. It was published in 1990 in A Tree Full of Leaves Which Are Stars, *an anthology of Native American student poetry edited by Mick Fedullo.*

The Desert

As I walk in the desert
I see a coral snake passing by,
and the bright sun shines the day.

I hear birds singing on a
mesquite tree. I hear animals
crying for food and water.

I feel a strong breeze passing by,
and the animals come to me
so I can touch them.

So, next time you are in
a desert, like me, see things,
feel things, and hear things.

*Eucario Mendez, a Yaqui from Arizona, wrote his poem
during sixth grade. It was published in 1990 in* A Tree
Full of Leaves Which Are Stars, *an anthology of Native
American student poetry edited by Mick Fedullo.*

A World Within a World

I live in a world within a world. My world consists of a proud Indian heritage. The other world is full of high technology, futuristic ideas, and huge corporations.

My world is called the reservation. It may not have fine hotels and penthouses, but who needs these things on a reservation? On the reservation, everyone is equal in some way or another. We have the same color skin, the same language, and the same beliefs.

Our tradition is important to us all. Without it, our ways of knowing how our ancestors lived long ago would have been extinct. I praise the elderly Native Americans who have tried to keep tradition and customs alive by telling and showing young people what we really are and not what non-Indians believe we should be.

Reservations are sometimes alienating because people are afraid of Indians. One misconception is that we are people of a low moral standard. Other misconceptions are sometimes a result of people watching too many westerns on television.

Every tribe is united with every other tribe because of one common bond: race. When a tribe is in dispute with the government or a corporation, I have no choice but to listen. The outcome can directly or indirectly affect the Native American way of life.

As the Choctaw tribe heads into the coming years,

we may leave the reservation, but we cannot relinquish our heritage. My heritage is something that will remain important to me until the day I die.

Brian Willis, a sixteen-year-old Mississippi Choctaw, wrote "A World Within a World" as an English assignment in 1991. The Mississippi Choctaw Reservation is located near Philadelphia, Mississippi.

Ritual and Ceremony

The rituals of every Indian community are essential to the continuation of life. Native Americans accord respect to those who have earned the right to participate in rituals that concern the spiritual life of the community. Non-Indians should not be offended when turned away from a ritual or ceremony. These activities are profoundly tied to the well-being of the performer, the recipient of the ceremony, and the community at large.

Most Native American groups across the United States celebrate Euramerican holidays in much the same manner as everyone else, but they have other rituals associated with harvests and the life-cycle events of birth, child naming, puberty, marriages, and death. Native American ritual behavior and activities typically include prayers for the health and well-being of all life.

These writings by Native young people reflect their early introduction to ritual and ceremony.

Old Man, the Sweat Lodge

"This small lodge is now
The womb of our mother, Earth.
This blackness in which we sit,
The ignorance of our impure minds.
These burning stones are
The coming of new life."
I keep his words near my heart.

Confessing, I recall my evil deeds.
For each sin, I sprinkle water on red-hot stones.
The hissed steam is a sign that
The place from which Earth's seeds grow
is still alive.
He sweats.
I sweat.

I remember, Old Man heals the sick,
Brings good fortune to one deserving.
Sacred steam rises;
I feel my pores give out their dross.
After I chant prayers to the Great Spirit,
I raise the door to the east.
Through this door dawns wisdom.

Cleansed, I dive into icy waters.
Pure, I wash away all of yesterday.
"My son, walk in this new life.
It is given to you.
Think right, feel right.
Be happy."
I thank you, Old Man, the Sweat Lodge.

[The sweat lodge, a place of worship and ceremony, is a central part of the religious beliefs of nearly all American Indian tribes. The sweat is a purification ritual regarded as a sacred rite in itself; it is sometimes part of a larger religious ceremony.]

Phil George, a Nez Percé born in Seattle, Washington, was nineteen years old when he wrote "Old Man, the Sweat Lodge." He was a student at the newly created Institute of American Indian Arts (IAIA) in Santa Fe, New Mexico. His poem was included in the IAIA Anthology of Poetry and Verse, published in 1965 by the Bureau of Indian Affairs.

Chili

On the Feast Day I will eat hot red chili
which is rough with meat
and some oven-baked hot light brown dough bread
the chili will taste hot, smooth, juicy, spicy
and the color of orange red
the bread with a light brown crust and a white inside
and the meat will be scrumptious
and juicy and very very good
and an icy cold red drink on a very hot day.

[Feast Day is a religious celebration that combines both Catholic and Native rituals. Each pueblo that has a day set aside for honoring its patron saint has an open house for guests, who are permitted to watch the ceremonies in the plaza and are invited to feast in Pueblo adobe houses on bowls of red and green chili, *posole*, stews, and oven bread. *Posole* is a southwestern corn soup; oven bread is baked in an outdoor adobe brick oven.]

Eugene Holgate, from Taos Pueblo, participated in a creative writing program organized in several Pueblo day schools by Randy Silva, an arts and crafts teacher then with the Northern Pueblos Agency, and Harold Littlebird, poet and artist. Eugene was in the fourth grade when his poem was published in 1980 in Beneath Rainbows, *a compilation of student works from the project.*

Prayer

I get up, eat and
say my morning
prayer. I walk to the
reddish mesa. It's one of the

colorful things I see.
By noon I get to the
mesa. I climb
to the top

And say my
midnoon prayer. I
start to cry, so I wipe
the tears out of my

eyes to see the
beauty in the nation.
I start to walk
home in beauty.

I get home and
eat and say my
evening prayer and
get in bed and

wait for tomorrow
to walk in beauty again.

Kermit Lee Yazzie, a Navajo, was a sixth-grade student who participated in a creative writing program at Chinle Boarding School in Chinle, Arizona. His poem was published in the 1987–1988 Chinle Boarding School Poetry Calendar.

Me and My People

As I walk to Peigan,
everything is cold
and bitter. I come to this
place every new year.
I use sweet grass and cedar.
I burn it and use the
smoke to bless everyone
in the new year, so they
will have a happy
and safe new year.
As I look
at my people, it's as if
I can feel their love and
caring desires for one
another. My people . . .
. . . . . . are one.

Janadele Baker, a member of the Crow Tribe in Montana, wrote her poem after working with Mick Fedullo, poet-in-residence at St. Charles Mission School. "Me and My People" was published in 1988 in In the New World, *an anthology of poetry by Crow students who attended St. Charles Mission and Pretty Eagle schools.*

Going up the Mountain

I ride my horse up the
mountain. As I'm riding,
I sing a traditional
song that I have just
learned.
Soon, I reach the top
of the mountain and look
down. I can see my
relatives playing and working.
I can see the houses
that are hidden behind
the hills. It looks
like I'm looking at a map.
The roads are going from
hogan to hogan.
I pray to the Great
Spirit up above.
I ask for good
peace and harmony.
I ride down
singing the same traditional
song.

*Jonavan Largo, a Navajo in eighth grade, wrote this
poem, which was published in the 1989–1990 Wingate*

Elementary School Poetry Calendar. *Edited by Mick Fedullo, the calendar project was part of a writing program he conducted at the school in Fort Wingate, New Mexico.*

The Run

Waking up to see darkness
then hearing a voice say Get up
I think then remember
time to run it is morning

Getting dressed I feel like
falling asleep but
I must not it's time to pray
time to run it's morning

We get some cornmeal
Pray says Grandfather
Pray to run like a deer now
So I pray to run like a deer

We see the sun come up
a big red sphere in the sky
The land is brown, red, then green
Green with trees and plants

Starting to run
up the mesa I go
the steam of my breath hitting my face
Keep running you can make it

Running to the ranch
down to the mesa to the canal
then stopping to get some water for I still
have six miles to go

Run I hear Grandfather's voice say
Go to the ranch then maybe
you can ride Blacky when you're through
Blacky, I say, got to run

Running you get tired
your legs start to throb
you feel like stopping but you mustn't
you're almost to the ranch

Run the ranch is just over the hill
At last I see the ranch
Blacky I also see Blacky
She lifts her head sees me coming.

[Running is vital to many Native American religions. The
Hopis and other Pueblo peoples perform ceremonial runs
especially around the solstices and equinoxes.]

*Rudy Tewawina, a Hopi student in the seventh grade,
wrote "The Run." It was published in 1990 in* A Tree
Full of Leaves Which Are Stars, *an anthology of Native
American student poetry compiled by Mick Fedullo.*

Education

Traditionally, Native parents, clan members, and elders taught children cultural values, religious beliefs, tribal history, and all they needed to know about their universe in order to live a balanced life. In the late 1800s, government officials forced Indian children to attend distant boarding schools. They were often physically dragged out of their homes against the will of their parents. Most boarding schools were intentionally located far from Indian communities. Children and families were deliberately separated for most of the school year so that the schools could erase the students' tribal cultures and replace them with the values of the non-Indian world.

For half the day, boarding-school teachers taught academic subjects—reading and writing the English language, arithmetic, geography, and U.S. history. Teachers punished students who used their Native languages. The other half of the day, the boys studied blacksmithing, harness making, and carpentry; the girls worked at sewing, cooking, canning, and doing the laundry. All the students learned farming.

From the moment the boys and girls woke up, they

were required to march, in military formations and in uniforms. Native clothes and hairstyles were strictly forbidden. The children marched to meals, marched to classes, marched in their free time. In many cases, children went to school in unused military installations, forts, and stockades.

For months at a time, Indian students were sent on "outing experiences" to live with white families, do their farm and household chores, become immersed in the English language, and absorb white, Christian values for the purpose of assimilation into white society.

Boarding school administrators encouraged students to write to family and friends. They were warned, however, to keep their letters cheerful and were cautioned not to mention homesickness and sadness.

Although from the 1920s to the 1940s there was growing criticism of off-reservation boarding schools from Red Cross investigators, educators, physicians, and other reformers, as well as long-standing opposition from Indian parents, Congress resisted closing the schools. Finally, in the 1950s, the federal budget planners shifted the emphasis from boarding schools to local public schools. Although most Indian students thereafter attended local schools, public school education also aimed to assimilate Indians. In the 1960s, when public opinion became more accepting of cultural pluralism, Congress authorized funds for Indian education and cultural programs. Numerous tribes and communities contracted with the Bureau of Indian Affairs (BIA) to manage their own schools with federal funds, established local school boards, set up alternative schools, and started developing culturally based curricula. Over the years, the government closed most of the off-reservation boarding schools. Today, only two remain open.

Ninety percent of Indian children now attend public schools. The remainder attend tribe-operated schools, mission schools, or BIA-operated day schools.

In the last twenty years, Indian people have gained some control over both BIA schools and public schools enrolling a majority of Indian students. They are insisting on culturally sensitive textbooks, curricula, and tests. Budget cuts, however, eliminate or threaten Indian initiatives.

Frank Keokuk, a Sac and Fox, was about seventeen years old when he wrote this letter describing his high school experience at Hampton Institute in Hampton, Virginia. Hampton was the first off-reservation, government-run boarding school, the forerunner of the system designed to assimilate Indians into the dominant society.

Dear Friend:

. . . and in the fall [of 1883] a gentleman by the name of Mr. Talbot came to the reservation after children to come here [to Hampton], and as I wanted to learn more I joined the party that bounded here. I find that the rules are very stricked [strict], but I hope that I can soon learn to go by the rules like any other boy here. I have been here two months. I am in the Advanced class in the Indian school. We study the following books: *The Appleton's Standard Geography*, the Arithmetic as far as division, Grammar, History, and the Story of the Bible. My work is on the farm, as the shops are all full. I work two days out of the week and go to school four days. The boys are all divided out into companies A, B, C, D. I am in the A Company. A Company drills every Tuesday evening after school. I like this place pretty well, but sometimes I get homesick, but I guess I will like it better the longer I stay here. . . . I will tell you my age. I am about seventeen years of age. I have a brother who is ten years of age. He will someday go to school here, I guess, if nothing happens, and if he wants to come.

Well, dear friend, I must bring my letter to a close now. . . .

Very respectfully yours,
Frank Keokuk

Frank Keokuk's letter was published in the Southern Workman *(published at Hampton from 1878 to 1925) in February 1887. Frank Keokuk was the great-grandson of Keokuk, an Indian leader during the early nineteenth century. Keokuk, Iowa, is named after him.*

Anna Bender, a Chippewa (or Ojibwa) from the White Earth Reservation, was about six years old when her parents sent her to the Lincoln Institute in Philadelphia in the late nineteenth century. She spent summers in the country near Valley Forge. After seven years, she returned to Minnesota. . . .

A Stranger

I had no reason for wanting to go home except that other students went to theirs. I seldom heard from my parents and was so young when I came away that I did not even remember them. . . .

How miserable I felt when the time came to go! It was to me the leaving of a home instead of returning to one. The trip was very pleasant at first for there was a crowd of us returning, but when we got to Chicago I was made sad and lonely again by the departure of my friends. From St. Paul I had to travel all alone, not for long as my home was just fifty miles from there.

My mother met me at the station bringing with her my two younger sisters and two younger brothers whom I had never seen. They greeted me kindly but they and everything being so new and strange that I burst into tears. To comfort me my mother took me into a store close by and bought me a bag of apples. As the house was only about a mile from the station we all walked home into the woods while my sisters tried to cheer me up by telling me about places we passed and the good times they had. . . .

As we gathered around the table later a great wave of homesickness came over me. I could not eat for the lump in my throat and presently I put my head down and cried good and hard, while the children looked on in surprise. When my father returned from work he greeted me kindly but scanned me from head to foot. He asked me if I remembered him and I had to answer no. He talked to me kindly and tried to help me recall my early childhood, but I had never known many men and was very shy of him. At last he told me I had changed greatly from a loving child to a stranger.

This excerpt is from Anna Bender's The Story of My Life, *her undated autobiography written before she graduated from Hampton Institute in 1906.*

Alvis M. Morrin, a Red Cliff Chippewa student from Bayfield, Wisconsin, born about 1896, was a 1914 graduate of Carlisle Indian School in Carlisle, Pennsylvania. Carlisle was opened in 1879 by Captain Richard Henry Pratt, who once wrote "To civilize the Indian, put him in the midst of civilization. To keep him civilized, keep him there." The goal of this off-reservation boarding school, which closed in 1918, was to assimilate Indian students into the American mainstream.

Opportunity

Here at Carlisle we are surrounded by countless opportunities—trade schools, books, teachers, athletic instruction, Christian and literary societies, friends interested in our progress. All are here to be converted into our opportunities. We have a great chance to fit ourselves for our lifework and prove to the world what our race is capable of doing, given opportunity for self-improvement. Canova, though a scullion in the palace, saw his chance, grasped the opportunity that came his way, and showed to the world what he could do. Why cannot we, who are free to enter upon any vocation and are surrounded by opportunities of which Canova never dreamed, become famous, too?

. . . Among our own race are men, handicapped at first, who have risen to the front. Dr. Eastman, born and reared in a wigwam and living in the wilds of the Indian country, fought his way upward and is now a well-known author and lecturer. Mr. Charles Curtis battled with obstacles and became a United States senator. Our lot is easier than theirs, for race prejudice has been overcome, and a beneficent Government is giving the Indian youth the opportunities which once belonged only to the white man. Open doors to any vocation are waiting for the Indian to enter.

[Antonio Canova was an eighteenth-century Italian sculptor. Charles Alexander Eastman, a Dakota born in 1858, who received a medical degree from Boston University, wrote and lectured extensively. Charles Curtis, a Kansa born in 1860, was admitted to the bar at twenty-one years of age. Elected to the United States Senate in 1906, he served there for twenty years. He was vice president of the United States from 1929 to 1933.]

These excerpts are from Alvis M. Morrin's article entitled "Opportunity" for the Carlisle Arrow Annual Senior Number, *edited by the graduating class of 1914.*

In 1932, Laura Siyuja, a Havasupai, was a student at Phoenix Indian School, an off-reservation boarding school in Arizona that opened in 1891 and closed in 1989. Laura, along with other Indian girls, was sent out to work in a white home. She described her experience, which took her to Los Angeles, California. . . .

My Outing Experience

In Los Angeles one sees many Indian girls working in homes. There is an outing field matron for the Indian girls. She places the girls in the homes. When I was in California, I wanted to learn more about how the people live so I went to work in one of the homes in Hollywood. As it was my first time to leave home I was very lonesome, wishing that I were home.

I never had done a great deal of work at home. Of course I had helped around the house but usually I spent my time playing. This house where I was working had four in the family. I had to be up at six o'clock in the morning to get the breakfast ready. After breakfast, I washed the dishes. Then I cleaned the kitchen, bedrooms, the sitting rooms, bathrooms, and halls. I took care of the children. I gave them a swim in the ocean when we went to the beach, and if we went to the parks, we swam in swimming pools.

The outing girls learn many things which help them

in schoolwork. If they are working in Los Angeles they can go to San Pedro to see the warships and visit the old missions there. It is very interesting to visit some places in California. One also becomes acquainted with girls from other tribes who happen to be working there. There are girls from Arizona, New Mexico, Oregon, California, South Dakota, and other states.

This essay was published December 3, 1932, in the Phoenix Indian School paper, the Phoenix Redskin.

If I Were a Pony

If I were a pony,
A spotted pinto pony,
A racing, running pony,
I would run away from school.
And I'd gallop on the mesa,
And I'd eat on the mesa,
And I'd sleep on the mesa,
And I'd never think of school.

*Navajo students at the Tohatchi School in New Mexico
made up the preceding poem as a group, with each child
furnishing a line, the whole poem being the result of a
talk among the group. "If I Were a Pony" was published
in the children's issue of* Indians at Work, *a government
publication, in the summer of 1933.*

In December 1967, a group of Lakota high school freshmen from Holy Rosary High School in Pine Ridge, South Dakota, submitted testimony to the Special Senate Subcommittee on Indian Education. The Lakota students gave their reactions to Acculturational Psychology, a new course introduced by Father John F. Bryde in September of 1966.

Something Really Different

Patrick Kills Crow and Mary Crazy Thunder: We've got something really different and exciting at Holy Rosary this year, and our whole class is talking about it. You'll probably be surprised when I say the exciting thing is a *New Class*, but that's what it is. I never thought that I would look forward to a class before, but we sure do now. Father Bryde went away and did a lot of studying, and when he came back, he started this new course.

When Father first came in and put the name of the new course on the board, we couldn't even pronounce it, much less know what it meant. It's called Acculturational Psychology, and it can also be called Modern Indian Psychology. It means a study of how to be a modern Indian. Since we are the same as the old-time Indians, except in our way of making a living now, we have to learn two things—how to be like the old-time Indians and yet make our living in a different way. Since this can be kind of hard, this thing called adjustment, we have to learn how. And that's what makes the course so interesting. No one ever told us this before.

Before this course, we didn't even know that Indians were important or that it was important for us to know Indian history and values and what the old-time Indians did hundreds of years ago. Now we can see that it is, and it sure makes you feel good to know that you are a Sioux. It makes you really proud to see all the obstacles the old-time Sioux had to overcome and to know that the Indian race is the oldest race on the face of the earth today. Father says this speaks well of our values because a people is only as long-lived as their values. . . .

[At the end of the term, students evaluated the course.]

Francis Clifford: This course means a lot to me because I learned about my own people. I know their values and many other great things about them. Now I am glad I'm an Indian. Before I was ashamed of it. . . .

Charlotte Zephier: After studying [Indian values] I found them quite interesting. I think if all Indians—I mean, kids and teenagers—had a course in this they wouldn't even be bothered by the dominant group anymore! It becomes a real help after being shut off by other people for *so long*.

Debi Rooks: This course in itself was something completely different from anything I've ever had before. . . . It enlightens a person such as myself to the real Indian ways, not just the jazz one watches on TV.

The TV is giving a misleading view of the Indian, and this, with other propaganda, is what is giving the Average American a twisted and warped image of the Indian. I think this course . . . should be taught to every American so they could derive a better understanding and be more proud of the Indian heritage.

Ernie Little: The most exciting part of your teaching was the part on the Sioux Indian Wars. And I'm sure all the class would agree. I bet no one was tardy for your class during this period. I know a lot about Indians now so I can speak for them when somebody talks about them. . . . I respect myself and others more now that I know the values and how the Indians acted long ago. . . .

Paul Herman, Jr.: Now that I know my values, I understand Indians more clearly, not to mention myself. I feel proud of myself and [my] forefathers. I feel more sure of myself when making decisions.

Seven volumes of testimony from hearings held by the Special Senate Subcommittee on Indian Education became the basis for a major study of Indian education titled Indian Education: A National Tragedy, a National Challenge, *published in 1969.*

Rising Voices

Way out in the heart of the reservation,
sand always blowing, tumbleweeds rolling,
the Navajos are gaining control of their destination.

Sheltered by Black Mountain,
whites and Navajos are striving to educate
with understanding and appreciation,
not defiance, scorn, or hate.

Trying to teach and learn side by side.
Bilingual and bicultural.
Will it work? Is it working?
Maybe . . . and maybe not.

But we people are giving it a try,
Trying to learn both ways,
Trying to be in harmony with both ways—
If only those outside will let us.

Our traditions survive;
Our heroes of legends and tribal history
are alive in what we learn.
So we can continue to tell our story.

Our cherished medicine men
have young trainees, so that when
the old ones are dead and gone,
the ceremonies for another generation
will live on.

What will be the result of this attempted peace?
I'll tell you this—listen!
From the silent, windswept land a voice can be
      heard.

Rising from the monolithic monuments,
purple mountains and rolling grasslands,
The moaning winds carry a soft
but steadily rising voice . . .

A voice made of many voices
of proud men and women
with a hope and a question. . . .
Will we make it? . . . Listen!

The Voice—our Voice—is getting
      stronger
Rising to the turquoise sky—
Listen! You will hear it soon . . .
very soon. . . .

*Carla Willetto, a Navajo at Rough Rock Community High
School in Arizona, wrote "Rising Voices" during the
1977–1978 school year. Her poem was published in 1982
in* Rough Stones Are Precious Too, *Vol. 2, a publication
of the Navajo Curriculum Center. Established in 1966,*

Rough Rock is renowned for being the first Indian-directed, locally controlled school using bilingual-bicultural texts. Its curriculum center still produces books about Navajo history and culture.

Harsh Realities

All people in the United States regularly see inauthentic, unrealistic, dishonest, offensive images of Indians. Learning materials, picture books, television, movies, comics, advertisements, games and toys, greeting cards, clothing, and food packages convey stereotyped messages about Indians. It is no surprise that Indian children who constantly see their people portrayed or treated in unfair ways begin to feel and act as if they are not as good as other people. With constant rejection by society, Indian youngsters soon learn to reject themselves. Native American parents and educators constantly speak out about this stereotyping because their children are victimized by poorly educated non-Indians brought up on a steady diet of distorted images. These images impede Indian parents and communities from raising their children with positive information about their heritage.

Besides battling discrimination, Indian peoples are still dealing with the legacy of compulsory federal boarding schools and other policies that tried to stamp out their cultures, languages, spiritual traditions, and histories. Tribal communities are struggling today to maintain their homelands and political sovereignty. Daily, they fight challenges to their religious beliefs; land, timber, mineral, and water rights; treaty-protected rights; and voting rights. Daily, Indian people battle high unemployment rates on reservations, high diabetes rates, low average life spans, and low self-esteem. Daily, Indian people struggle with alcohol and drug abuse. Daily, Indians struggle to reconcile traditional views with the values of the non-Indian world.

Many young Indians, well aware of the social, economic, and political problems facing Indian communities, have responded with poetry and prose.

That They Might Have Their Rights

How is it that some people say that Indians don't like to work; I'd like to know if they have been among them and have given them things to work with, such as plows and wagons. . . . [T]hen they write things about them, saying that "they don't like to work but like to fight." . . . [Indians] have been treated bad and have been driven away from their homes and tried to stand for their rights; then they say they like to fight, but still they mind whatever the government tells them to do; they don't go and gather Indian warriors to have a war between the whites, but they wait for the government to give them the implements to work with, for they cannot till the soil with their fingernails. Especially my tribe, the Pawnees, they never had trouble with the whites as long as I can remember. . . . The whites have nearly all the land now which belonged to the Indians, and have killed all the animals which they used to live upon, and left them in the darkness. . . . And I think it is time that every tribe of Indians ought to have a new treaty with the government and make it as fair as they can . . . that they might have their rights as any other nation has, in the United States. And I hope when General Garfield occupies the Presidency that some Indians will make a new treaty with the government.

In January 1881, when he was about eighteen years old, James R. Murie, or Young Eagle, a Pawnee who later worked for the Field Museum in Chicago, reacted to stereotyping of Indians by non-Indians and expressed his feelings about the mistreatment of his people. "That They Might Have Their Rights" appeared in the Southern Workman, *published at Hampton Institute, then a boarding school for Indian and African-American students in Hampton, Virginia.*

New Way, Old Way

Beauty in the old way of life
The dwellings they decorated so lovingly;
A drum, a clear voice singing,
And the sound of laughter.

You must want to learn from your mother,
You must listen to old men
   not quite capable of becoming white men.
The white man is not our father.
While we last, we must not die of hunger.
We were a very Indian, strong, competent people,
But the grass had almost stopped its growing,
The horses of our pride were near the end.

Indian cowboys and foremen handled Indian herds.
A cowboy's life appealed to them until
   economics and tradition clashed.
No one Indian was equipped to engineer the water's
      flow
   onto a man's allotment.
Another was helpless to unlock the gate.
The union between a hydroelectric plant and
Respect for the wisdom of the long-haired chiefs
   had to blend to build new enterprises
By Indian labor.

Those mighty animals graze once more upon the
     hillside.
At the Fair appear again our ancient costumes.
A full-blood broadcasts through a microphone
     planned tribal action.
Hope stirs in the tribe,
Drums beat and dancers, old and young, step forward.

We shall learn all the devices of the white man.
We shall handle his tools for ourselves.
We shall master his machinery, his inventions,
     his skills, his medicine, his planning;
But we'll retain our beauty
And still be Indians!

*Dave MartinNez, a Navajo student at the Institute of
American Indian Arts in Santa Fe, New Mexico, wrote
"New Way, Old Way" in a creative writing class during
the early 1960s. It was published in 1965 in* Anthology
of Poetry and Verse, *a Bureau of Indian Affairs publication.*

A Telegram

A telegram arrived yesterday
  About my brother
    Wounded in Vietnam.
      Nothing else.
        Nothing about
          time or
            place.
              Just a short apology.

My mother cried for Jesus
  My father fainted when he heard
    I had never seen him so scared.

We sat quietly,
  Trying to avoid the sadness
  Written on each of our faces.
  Thinking of my brother,

    Their son,
    Across the ocean

    In a war
      Brought home to our aching hearts.

At night
  I feel lonely
  with my father's silence

  and my mother's tears.

Nora Naranjo Morse, a member of Santa Clara Pueblo, wrote "A Telegram" in 1968 when she was fifteen years old and living in Taos, New Mexico, with her parents. This poem reflects the experiences of many Native people during the Vietnam War.

Indians

Indians are native people
    here before the Pilgrims came
    here before Columbus came
    here before the Vikings came
Yet, we are treated
As though we don't belong here
Indians are native people
    here before the Pilgrims came
    here before Columbus came
    here before the Vikings came
Yet, we are treated
As though we just got here.

Ophelia Rivas, a Tohono O'odham eighth-grade student at Santa Rosa School in Arizona, wrote a contest-winning poem. "Indians" was submitted to the judges of the Creative Writing Project, a BIA-funded project whose purpose was to provide American Indian students with opportunities to express themselves in writing. Her poem was published in Arrow III *in 1971.*

Going into Space

SO I GUESS THEY ARE GOING INTO DAMN
        SPACE AGAIN SOON.

A TWO AND A HALF BILLION DOLLAR
        CAMPING TRIP.

OH SURE THESE THREE HAVE ACCOMPLISHED
        MUCH IN THEIR LIVES.

THEIR BOY SCOUTING WILL FINALLY
        COME INTO A REAL TEST

WHY DON'T THEY HOVER THEIR SPACECRAFT
        OVER THE RESERVATIONS

OR HOVER THEIR SCREAMING STEEL OVER
        THE GHETTOS AND SEE

BUT I GUESS YOU CANNOT SEE THE POVERTY
        FROM 28 MILES ABOVE THE EARTH.

Francis Becenti, a Navajo, wrote this poem in 1971 when he was nineteen years old.

In Indian Country

. . . I've got three brothers and two sisters. We all moved to Manchester, Connecticut, in September of 1967. We went down because of the work. That's why my parents went down. I didn't want to go down at all, but I was underage and my mother told me back then— I was kinda rowdy, always getting in trouble—she'd worry about me and she'd feel a lot better if I went down, so I says, "Okay, I'll go down and I'll try to go back to school and see how it is."

We got there a week before school opened, and I went in first day. Down there they have to be all dressed up in school. Coming from Maine, I had on jeans and a jersey, just the way I always went to school. I go walking in, and I see all these kids just looking at me like I was a freak or something. I went in one class and sat down, and the teacher introduced me. She said, "Well, we have a new student. His name is Martin Neptune; he's a Penobscot Indian," like that, and everybody turns around and just stares at me. I really felt like a freak down there. In the second class they did the same thing. In the third class I saw the teacher; she turned around and looked at me; she says, "Oh yeah, we have a new student—" As soon as she said that, I walked right out; I didn't go back there again.

I couldn't understand it. They called the teams at the

school the Manchester Indians. That's what they have on their basketball suits, and there wasn't an Indian at all in that school. The same here in Old Town. Just recently they put that banner up in Old Town High School in the gym—YOU'RE IN INDIAN COUNTRY—and there's hardly any Indian kids that go out for any teams in that school. Maybe a couple'll go out for baseball; once in a while one will go out for track. Very few finish school. I heard there was something like a 90-percent dropout rate between the two reservations, Passama-quoddy and Penobscot.

Martin Neptune, a Penobscot from Maine, was twenty-one years old when he was interviewed by Peter Anastas. The interview was published in Glooskap's Children: Encounters with the Penobscot Indians of Maine, *published in 1973.*

Untitled

Vanishing era, my ancient past
      I want to know
if you exist or
      do your spirits still cast
and live in the shadows
      of the old ones.

Echoing spirits
      you, my people
who have gone
      and left upon
ancient canoes,
      one day you shall
return to your people.

My soul is lost
      as my heart listens
to its own beat
      it cries for the old ones
for they are slowly dying.
      It's a damn shame.

Tradition thrives
      within the old ones
the spirit still dances

and sings in temple
to the beating drums,
        they haven't forgotten
who they are.

Our young voices
        one cannot hear
who is to blame?
        the whiteman
and his way
        or ourselves?

Who has taken away
        our mother tongue,
was it John Wayne?

Our language is dying
        as the old ones
one by one leave
        to join the canoes
to the other side.

Tell me
        who's to blame,
me and you
        my people
or the whaneetum?

*Yvonne Thomas, from the Lummi Tribe in the state of
Washington, wrote ''Untitled'' while a student at the*

Institute of American Indian Arts in Santa Fe, New Mexico. Her poem was published in 1977 in Newborn, *an IAIA student publication.*

Come Brothers and Sisters

Come brothers and sisters
join the circle
give me your hands
throw away the bottle
which is poison
and destroys
our people
throw away the needle
which poisons our blood
and destroys our minds
throw away the weed
which makes us lazy
and with those
throw away hate and greed
and envy
which has destroyed
our people from the beginning
come brothers and sisters
join the sacred circle of life

*This poem by Eve Zamora, a Chippewa student at the
Heart of the Earth Survival School in Minneapolis, Minnesota, was published in 1979 in* Angwamas Minosewag Anishinabeg: Time of the Indian. *It was written*

during a writer-in-residence program David Martinson conducted on reservations and in urban centers for the Minnesota Chippewa Tribe.

We Shall Wait Forever

Back in the past
we, the ancestors, ruled the
quiet lands.
We would sit around camp fires
and sing with harmony.
The beating of the drums sounded
like the heart of an Indian. The cry
of a wolf, the howl of an owl, put us
into the secrets of ourselves.
Then we woke in the early mist of May,
and found ourselves in front
of our enemies, who had come to fight.
The children cried, the women ran
and hid. The men who were brave
stood up for us.
We fought, but many of us died.
Our spirits now haunt
the lands we walked on.
Now we sing, laugh, dance, and lie
under the bright blue sky. We are waiting
for our enemies who killed us to pass by.
We shall stay here and wait until
we find them. Until then we shall wait
in peace and harmony.

Darlene Sinyella, a Hualapai, wrote her poem during seventh grade at the Hualapai Elementary School in Peach Springs, Arizona. She participated in a special creative writing program at the school. "We Shall Wait Forever" was published in 1990 in A Tree Full of Leaves Which Are Stars, *an anthology of Native American student poetry edited by Mick Fedullo.*

We Will Never Forget . . .

The Great Sachem of the Gay Head Aquinnahs once said, "We will adopt those parts of the white man's culture that are best for us, and do so only gradually."

It is said that Mittark held to that statement and that Gay Head survived as an Indian Community longer than any other Wampanoag community.

Hiacombes was one of the first Indians to adopt the Whiteman's ways. He was the first Indian to convert and become a minister. His conversion was described as rather quick and he was put down by many of his people, who often referred to him as the "English man." Hiacombes was a Wampanoag from Great Harbor, now called Edgartown, where a few English families first settled in 1642. He was a Sannop (lowborn) of the tribes. . . .

Hiacombes, to me, represented the negative. Indians have always been taught to live positively and to think positively and not negatively. This to me meant Hiacombes wasn't a true Indian. An example of a true and positive Indian would be Epenowe, a native of this Island who was taken to Spain to be sold as a slave. After some time in England, Epenowe devised a means of escape (Epenowe convinced his capturers of a gold mine back on Capawack [the Indian name for Martha's Vineyard]). When they arrived back on Martha's Vineyard, he made a heroic escape back to his land and his people, proving himself a true Indian.

Today Indians around the country face the problem of whether to live the life of a traditional Indian or live the life of the Whiteman. There is a difference. Traditional Indians believe in keeping our old ways, living like the old people of the past. And then there are Indians that say, "Give up Indian ways," forget them and enjoy what the Whiteman has brought us, like stereos, televisions, cars, and modern homes. It is Indian people like Hiacombes that have forgotten Indian ways and have chosen to live in the Whiteman's society; they are the ones that have forgotten that the Whiteman has also brought us disease and poverty.

Hiacombes was what some Indians would call an apple—red on the outside but white on the inside. Hiacombes was always agreeing with the Whiteman and because of this it is said he was well thought of by the English and the Indians, but I found that the traditional Indians never cared about him. And I certainly know that the whites didn't either, since all Indians were considered savages, and this is proven in the letters and documents written by the Whitemen of that time. . . . The diseases that the Whiteman brought killed many Indian people. When Indians saw how Hiacombes converted and his family was untouched by the diseases, many of them converted. If anything, Hiacombes weakened his people. Because of Hiacombes, many Indians threw down their traditions and customs and gave up their beliefs, their culture. . . .

To me, it is the Whiteman's religion that should have been questioned. Everything I find in the Whiteman's society is based on religion and it's corrupt. Oh yes, I go to Whiteman's schools . . . I have learned to read from schoolbooks, newspapers, and even some of the bible; but in time, I have found that these were not enough. Civilized people depend too much on man-made printed pages. I turn to the Creator's book, which is the whole of his creation. You can read a big part of that book if you study nature. You know, if you take all your books, lay them out under the sun and let the snow and rain and insects work on them for a while, there will be nothing left of those books. I have been taught that the Great Spirit has provided you and me with an opportunity for study in nature's university: the forests, the rivers, the mountains, and the animals, which include us. . . .

Indians believe that everything has a purpose. So, it appears that we need people like Hiacombes to show us *how not to be*. By the same token, we need people like Epenowe to show us how to be true and strong. And, we need the Whiteman . . . who doesn't understand. The Whiteman from Europe, who is still a foreigner, a man who has hurt us deeply, but has shown us how not to be. The Whiteman has attempted to take our land, our culture, and our pride.

Although we understand that there are good white people, just like there are good Indians and bad Indians, and the same for all the other races, it must be understood that times have not changed that much. We Indians also understand that the Whiteman is continuing to take what little we have left today, but through education taken in by us native people and the practice of our ancient ways, he will continue to fail. It is for these

122

reasons that we Indians understand that those difficult times are not entirely over. . . . We will never forget.

Cameron J. Cuch, a sixteen-year-old Ute-Wampanoag student from Gay Head, Massachusetts, was one of forty-four students who entered an essay contest sponsored by the Dukes County Historical Society of Edgartown, Massachusetts. He received Honorable Mention for his paper, written in March 1991.

Acknowledgments

Grateful acknowledgment is made to the following for permission to reprint unpublished and copyrighted material.

Janadele Baker for "Me and My People."

Alan Barlow for "My Poems."

Beacon Press for "In Indian Country" by Martin Neptune from *Glooskap's Children* by Peter Anastas, copyright © 1973. Reprinted by permission of Beacon Press.

Neal Beaumont for "Under One Sun."

Francis Becenti for "Going into Space."

Willis Belin for "The Navajo Land."

Elliot Bryant for "My Late Grandfather."

Cameron J. Cuch for "We Will Never Forget."

Hampton University Archives for "A Stranger" by Anna Bender, "Dear Friend" by Frank Keokuk, and "That They Might Have Their Rights" by James R. Murie. Reprinted by courtesy of Hampton University Archives.

Havasupai Tribe for "We Are the Many" by Ingrid Putesoy and "Gifts" by Michelle Whatoname.

James Henry for "My Grandfather."

Eugene Holgate for "Chili."

Jessica Ahmsaty Hugo for "As I See" by Jessica Ahmsaty.

Benjamin Hunch for "About Grandma."

Katie Mobeck Johnson for "Misconceptions about the Aleutians" by Katie Mobeck.

Renae Kemp for "Longing."

Jonavan Largo for "Going up the Mountain."

Craig Magpie for "I Have a Dream."

Glory Thompson Maki for "Indian" by Glory Thompson.

Eucario Mendez for "The Desert."

Minnesota Chippewa Tribe for "Susan" by Thomas Headbird, "As I Walk This Road" by Ricardo Rojas, and "Come Brothers and Sisters" by Eve Zamora.

Nora Naranjo Morse for "A Telegram."

Glafiro Perez for "Yaqui Hopes."

Shandin Pete for "Grandpa."

Len Plenty for "The Bighorn River."

Lillian Rainer for "Apache People and Their Heritage."

Kimberly Kai Rapada for "My Role as a Native American."

Red School House for "To Be an Indian" by Murray Stonechild.

Rough Rock School Board for "A Trail Not Yet Finished" by Priscilla Badonie, "Rising Voices" by Carla Willetto, and "A Message" by Jennifer Yazzie.

San Juan School District, Montezuma Creek Elementary School for "Canyons" by Andrew Jones.

Darlene Sinyella for "We Shall Wait Forever."

Delia Spotted Bear for "My Family."

Misty Stands in Timber for "As I Walk along the Hillside."

Rudy Tewawina for "The Run."

United States Department of the Interior, Bureau of Indian Affairs Public Affairs Office for "Uncertain Admission" by Frances Bazil, "Bison" by Tonye Garter, "Old Man, the Sweat Lodge" by Phil George, "Gah-Chac-Ah" by Cecil Johnson, Jr., "My Tribe" by James Latone, "New Way, Old Way" by Dave MartinNez, "Indians" by Ophelia Rivas, "The Help Rain Gives Me" by Ethel Patkotak, "A Visit to Grandmother" by Vernida Polacca, "My Outing Experience" by Laura Siyuja, "It Is Not!" by Special Navajo Program, Phoenix Indian School, "Untitled" by Yvonne Thomas, and "If I Were a Pony" by Tohatchi School, New Mexico.

United States Department of the Interior, Indian Arts and Crafts Board for "Grammas Are Good" by Virgil Yellow Cloud.

Autumn White Clay for "As I Dance."

Brian Willis for "A World Within a World."

Wingate High School, Fort Wingate, New Mexico, for "I'm a Navajo" by Maggie Bahe and "Shi-ma-sani and Shi-cheeh" by Peggy Yazzie.

Kermit Lee Yazzie for "Prayer."

The authors give special thanks to the following people who supported their work: Juanita Claw, David Germany, Art Hobson, Bruce Hucko, John Langenbrunner, George Leong, Denise Low, Sharon Lynn, Karen and Kit McIlroy, Sol Padilla, Carl Shaw, Tammy Singer, Marlene Walking Bear, Lucille Watahomigie, and Carole Willis.

Author/Title Index